AT the ELEVENTH HOUR

And Other Expressions about MONEY and NUMBERS

BRIDGET HEOS

Illustrated by

AARON BLECHA

Lerner Publications Company

MINNEAPOLIS

Lerner Publications Company
A division of Lerner Publishing Group, Inc.
241 First Avenue North
Minneapolis, MN 55401 U.S.A.

Website address: www.lernerbooks.com

Library of Congress Cataloging-in-Publication Data

Heos, Bridget.
    At the eleventh hour : and other expressions about money and numbers / by Bridget Heos.
        p.   cm. — (It's just an expression)
    Includes index.
    ISBN 978-0-7613-8164-8 (lib. bdg. : alk. paper)
    1. English language—Idioms—Juvenile literature.
    2. Figures of speech—Juvenile literature. I. Title.
    PE1460.H46 2013
    428.1—dc23   2011044561

Manufactured in the United States of America
1 – PC – 7/15/12

TABLE of CONTENTS

INTRODUCTION

The students in Mrs. Cho's class are **on cloud nine.** They found out at **the eleventh hour** that they sold more cookies at the school bake sale than any other class. The class had spent **a pretty penny** on sprinkles and other decorations to make their cookies look great. They'd gone **the whole nine yards** to have the fanciest and tastiest treats at the sale. All their hard work was finally paying off. Mrs. Cho announced that they were going to have a party to celebrate their success!

Cloud nine? Eleventh hour? Pretty penny? Whole nine yards? What the heck is going on? Nothing you won't get once you get clued into the world of idioms. <u>Idioms are phrases that mean something different from what they seem to mean.</u> Often these phrases can seem super confusing. But once you learn what idioms mean—and where these phrases come from—they won't seem so bizarre after all. So read on if idioms have *you* at **sixes and sevens**!

ON CLOUD NINE

Lily's friend Brooklyn sat next to her on the bus. "I got the part!" she squealed. "I'm going to be Annie in the school play!" Lily hugged her. Then Brooklyn lounged back and stared at the bus ceiling, "I'm on cloud nine," she sighed.

Lily knew her friend was happy. But what exactly did she mean when she said she was on cloud nine? The phrase had to mean something good—right?

Yes! **Being on cloud nine means you're really happy.** It means that almost nothing can get in the way of your good mood. But where did this saying come from? Why don't people say they're on cloud eight? Or cloud one million, for that matter?

Cloud nine may be a meteorology term. Meteorology is the study of weather. Supposedly, old meteorology guides assigned a number to each different type of cloud. A cloud type called cumulonimbus was known as the ninth type of cloud. Cumulonimbus clouds are very pretty and float high in the sky. So if you felt like you were on cloud nine, you'd feel very high indeed!

GOODY TWO-SHOES

Kara came to school one day to find her teacher absent. "We're having a sub!" Ravi told her excitedly. "And we're all going to switch seats before she gets here so she can't tell who's who. It'll be awesome."

Some of Kara's classmates were already sitting in the wrong spots. But Kara took her seat in row three as usual. "I'm not going to sit someplace else," she said. "I don't want to get in trouble."

"Goody Two-shoes!" Ravi shouted.

What did Ravi mean by that? Kara knew that he was teasing her because she wouldn't trick the sub. But what did shoes have to do with anything?

The girls on the left won't have anything to do with their crazy classmates' troublemaking!

Very prim and proper kids might get labeled Goody Two-shoes.

Goody-Two-shoes means somebody who always follows the rules. You might even say a Goody Two-shoes is *annoyingly* good! The phrase comes from a children's story called *The History of Little Goody Two-Shoes.* Published in 1766, the story tells of a poor girl named Margery Meanwell who wanders the streets of London, England, wearing only one shoe. Then a kind soul gives her a matching shoe. She proudly shows everybody, exclaiming: "Two shoes! Two shoes!" People are so impressed by her gratitude and goodness that they give her other gifts. Eventually, she becomes a wealthy lady.

In the 1700s and 1800s, parents presented Goody Two-shoes as a role model. They asked their children, "Why can't you be more like Goody Two-shoes?" Naturally, children came to dislike her! That's why, these days, people who won't break even the slightest little rule might get labeled a Goody Two-shoes.

At SIXES and SEVENS

Keith had a bad cold and missed three days of school. When he came back to class, he was having trouble understanding the story that his teacher assigned to his reading group. "I don't know some of the words in the story," he admitted nervously to his teacher.

Mr. Shields could tell that Keith felt bad. "Oh, Keith, this story has you at sixes and sevens, doesn't it?" he said. "But don't worry. It includes words that are new to everybody. We learned some new vocabulary terms while you were gone. The story uses those terms, so we just have to get you caught up on what they mean." Keith is glad that his teacher doesn't seem angry. He's also relieved to hear that he's not expected to know all the words in the story. But what does Mr. Shields mean by *at sixes and sevens?* Is it OK to be at sixes and sevens? Or is this one more thing Keith has to worry about?

This kid looks totally confused. You might say his tricky assignment has him at sixes and sevens!

Sixes and sevens describes a state of confusion. Keith doesn't have to feel nervous—the state will pass just as soon as he gets caught up in reading. Besides, we're *all* at sixes and sevens at one time or another. But just where does this phrase come from?

According to a popular legend, it comes from two craftsmen's guilds (groups made up of people who do similar jobs) in London, England. The groups were the Merchant Taylors, who made clothes, and the Skinners, who worked with animal skins and pelts. London had many craftsmen's guilds. They often argued over their place in the order of precedence (an official ranking based on the year that they were established). Disagreements between the Merchant Taylors and the Skinners were especially heated. The Merchant Taylors claimed that they were sixth in the order of precedence. But the Skinners insisted that *they* were sixth. They couldn't settle the argument, and it went on for years! In 1484 the mayor of London finally ruled that the groups would alternate the sixth position every year.

These days, we use the phrase *at sixes and sevens* when someone's confused or just doesn't seem to be getting anywhere. It's not too fun to be at sixes and sevens. If you find yourself in this state, hopefully it will pass quickly—just as it did for Keith when Mr. Shields reviewed the new vocab words with him.

SIX DEGREES of SEPARATION

Maya asked Hunter what he was doing after school. "I'm going downtown," he said. "My mom's taking me to this huge art supply store to pick up some poster board and other stuff for that project we're doing in art next week."

"Hey, say hi to my brother for me," replied Maya. "He works downtown."

Hunter laughed. "Him and about a million other people. I'm *sure* we'll bump into each other."

Hunter called Maya at home that night. "Guess what?" he said. "I didn't see your brother, but I met his girlfriend! She was working at the art supply store."

"Woah," said Maya. "That's like six degrees of separation."

What does Maya mean by that? **Six degrees of separation just means that everybody is closely connected.** It's another way of saying that it's a small world—or a world where we're all intertwined.

Talk to enough people and you're bound to find someone who's separated from you by six degrees!

How did the expression get its start? In the 1960s, psychologist Stanley Milgram conducted an experiment. He asked some Nebraskans to deliver documents to a stranger in Boston, Massachusetts. Each person was to send the documents to an acquaintance (somebody that he or she knew). The acquaintances would keep passing the documents on to other acquaintances until they reached the man in Boston. <u>In many cases, the documents were never delivered. But when they were delivered, it took only about six people to get them to the Boston man.</u> The conclusion was that we're separated from strangers by only about six steps, or degrees. Psychologist Judith Kleinfeld later questioned the conclusion since so many documents were undelivered. But the idea stuck.

So exactly how closely are we *really* connected to others? No one knows for sure. But we do know that the more friendly and talkative you are, the more likely you are to have lots of "six degree" moments!

Chatty, friendly people find themselves in lots of "six degree" situations.

BACK to SQUARE ONE

Delaney and Luis were building a volcano cake for a science project. The directions said to cut a hole in the center of the cake. Then they were to place baking soda in the hole. Next, they were supposed to mix cherry gelatin and lemon juice together and pour the mixture into the center of the cake. The volcano would erupt.

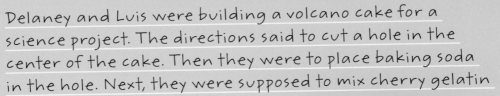

But Luis got hungry. He ate a piece of cake. Delaney saw him. She cut a piece for herself too. Now the volcano was ruined. "Guess it's back to square one," Delaney said.

What did Delaney mean? *Back to square one* means "back to the beginning." People often say this when a project goes wrong and they have to start over.

Mmmmm...volcano cake. It looks way too tasty to be a science project!

The expression probably refers to a board game. In many games, players move forward square by square. If they land on an unlucky square, they move backward. They may even have to go back to the beginning, or square one. One such board game is called Snakes and Ladders. It was invented long ago in India. In the game, players roll the dice. <u>If they land on a ladder square, they climb to the top. If they land on a snake's head, they slide to the bottom.</u> In the United States, this game was redesigned as a popular board game you've probably heard of—Chutes and Ladders.

A Snakes and Ladders game board

The WHOLE NINE YARDS

It was taco salad day in the lunchroom. Yum! But Owen was annoyed by classmates who held up the line with special requests. "No tomatoes on mine," said Gudahi. "Extra hamburger," said Hannah. "No lettuce," insisted Ashley.

No lettuce? It was a *salad*. When it was Owen's turn, he kept it simple. "I'll take the whole nine yards, please," he said.

What did Owen mean by *the whole nine yards?* He was using an expression, of course! **The whole nine yards** means **all of something.** Owen wanted all the ingredients on his taco salad. The whole nine yards can also mean that you're going all out, or doing all you can.

The phrase's origin is unclear. Some think it's related to fabric. The whole nine yards could be the order for a large wedding veil, for instance.

This bride's veil just might be 9 yards (8 meters) long.

Others think the saying has to do with concrete. A concrete truck can hold approximately 9 cubic yards (7 cu. m). So if you needed a truck full of concrete, you could order the whole nine yards.

Nine is a popular number in phrases. We saw it before in the phrase *cloud nine*. And *dressed to the nines* means "dressed finely," as for a special occasion. Beginning in the late 1700s, the phrase *the nines* meant "excellent." This may be because nine is the highest single digit. *Nine lives* refers to the number of lives a cat supposedly has. The phrase dates at least to William Shakespeare's time. It's easy to see why people might've thought that cats had nine lives. Cats are wily and tough and usually manage to land on their feet.

So why does the number nine show up so much in expressions? No one knows for sure. It may just be that nine is a likable number!

This guy's dressed to the nines. The number nine appears in all kinds of expressions!

THE ELEVENTH HOUR

Luke stuffed his language arts book into his backpack. He knew he'd need it tonight to study for the huge language arts test tomorrow. "Don't wait until the eleventh hour to study for tomorrow's test," Mr. Lang cautioned his students just before the final bell rang. "Remember, the test will be a big part of your grade."

Eleventh hour? Luke thought to himself. *I might have to study for eleven whole hours if I want to pass this crazy test—but what does it mean to wait till the eleventh hour? Which hour is the eleventh hour, anyway?*

The eleventh hour just means the last minute. The saying comes from a parable (a story meant to teach) in the Bible. The parable is called "The Workers in the Vineyard." In this story, a landowner

Yikes! This kid just realized it's almost bedtime and he hasn't started studying for his test yet.

hires some workers at dawn. He hires others late in the morning. He hires still others at "the eleventh hour." This means the final hour in the workers' twelve-hour workday. All the workers are paid the same amount. Some workers think this is unfair. Why should those who started working at the eleventh hour get as much pay as those who'd started earlier in the day? But the landowner sticks to his payment system.

The point of the story isn't about work hours. It's about being rewarded for choosing to live your life in a way that's honorable and fair. The parable is saying that it doesn't matter *when* people start living honorably—as long as they start sometime. Regardless of when they start, they will be rewarded.

If you wait till the eleventh hour to start your homework, you might be in for a tough day at school.

A PRETTY PENNY

As class representative, Juan reported his classmates' ideas to the student council. Landon suggested getting an outdoor Ping-Pong table for the playground. Juan thought that sounded great. He brought up the idea at the next meeting. The student council president said, "That would cost a pretty penny. How on Earth would we pay for it?"

Juan wasn't exactly sure what *a pretty penny* meant. But he was pretty sure it meant they probably wouldn't be getting a Ping-Pong table anytime soon.

Equipment for games and sports often costs a pretty penny.

A pretty penny means "a lot of money." How did the phrase come to mean this? To find out, we have to go back to the year 1257. Back then, a gold piece worth one pound was issued in England. (These days, a pound is similar in value to the U.S. dollar.) It was a beautiful coin, but very few were made. Finding the rare coin was good luck. *Pretty penny* probably refers to that coin.

Pennies appear in several other phrases too. *Pennies from heaven* means unexpected financial luck. A *penny for your thoughts* is a phrase people use when they want to find out what someone else is thinking about. *A penny-pincher* is someone who often uses coupons and other savings methods. Penny-pinchers might even seem reluctant to spend any money at all.

The student council president, it turns out, is a penny-pincher. She tells the class representatives that there's *no way* the school can afford a Ping-Pong table. But then Chloe, another class representative, offers a suggestion. "Maybe we could hold a dance next month and charge everyone two dollars to get in," she says. "That would help pay for the Ping-Pong table."

"Awesome idea!" says Juan. Pretty penny or no, it looks as if the Ping-Pong table idea is back on after all.

BET YOUR BOTTOM DOLLAR

Tanya wanted to go sledding. But the hill behind her house was covered with brown grass instead of snow. It seemed as if Tanya would never get a chance to try out her new sled.

As Tanya moped in front of the window, her grandpa said, "Cheer up, Tanya! Just look at that sky. Snow is on the way. I can tell. You can bet your bottom dollar that we'll have plenty of snow for sledding by tomorrow morning."

Tanya was happy that her grandpa thought it was going to snow. He was usually right about these things. But she didn't know why he was telling her to bet—and she had no clue what a bottom dollar might be.

If a person bets his bottom dollar, it means he thinks he has a great chance of winning!

**Bet your bottom dollar means that you can be sure
something is going to happen.** The phrase dates to the Wild
West. There, poker players bet silver dollars. They stacked the coins
in front of them. If they pushed a whole stack forward, they
were betting all their money, down to the bottom dollar.

These days, silver dollars aren't quite as common as they were
in the Wild West. But the phrase *bet your bottom dollar* has stuck
around. Tanya almost wished she *had* bet her bottom dollar when
she woke up the next morning. The ground was blanketed with
snow. She grabbed her sled and hurried out the door, pausing only
to shout, "Grandpa, you were right!"

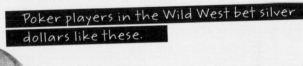

Poker players in the Wild West bet silver
dollars like these.

21

PAY the PIPER

On Thursdays, Nick, Lue, Mason, and Aidan stopped for ice cream after school. Lue's brother Toua worked behind the counter. The last two weeks, the boys had no money. Toua said they could pay at the end of the month, after they got their allowances.

*B*ut he was worried he'd get in trouble. He told his boss about it. She said that all customers needed to pay up front. That afternoon, Toua held out his palm as soon as the boys opened the door. "It's time to pay the piper," he said.

Lue knew his brother meant they had to pay up. But he didn't know why Toua was talking about a piper. What the heck did Toua mean?

The phrase *pay the piper* is based in part on an older phrase, *"Always those that dance must pay*

Treats like ice cream don't come free. To enjo a tasty bite, you have to pay up!

the musicke." This phrase appears in *Taylor's Feast*, a 1638 book by John Taylor. The phrase is also inspired by the fairy tale *The Pied Piper of Hamelin.* In that story, a character called the pied piper leads rats away from the town of Hamelin by playing music on his magic pipe. When the townspeople refuse to pay him, he leads the children away too.

Both the John Taylor phrase and the story of the pied piper mean that you have to face the consequences of your actions. If you dance, you have to pay the person providing the music. If you accept help from someone, you should repay him or her. And if you enjoy ice cream, you need to pay for that too.

Lue and his friends returned half an hour later with a pile of coins from their piggy banks. It was enough to pay the money they owed and to buy a single scoop of ice cream to split four ways. They would have to wait until they got their allowances to buy any more ice cream.

This artwork is from the story *The Pied Piper of Hamlin.*

BOUGHT the FARM

Ethan's great-grandpa was a pilot in World War II (1939–1945). He also taught other World War II soldiers how to fly. He showed Ethan his wedding photo. In it, his nose was bandaged. That morning, he'd been teaching somebody to fly. The student had lost control of the plane. "We almost bought the farm," he told Ethan.

A wedding? A crash landing? What did buying a farm have to do with any of this? Not much, it may seem—**until you know that bought the farm is an expression that means "died."**

The phrase *bought the farm* is something that men in the armed forces said during World War II. There are several stories about where the phrase came from. One story says that many soldiers talked about buying a farm after the war. They hoped

to settle down and raise a family there. <u>When they died, their friends would say, "He finally bought the farm," meaning that the war was over for the dead soldier and that he was finally at peace.</u>

Another story says that soldiers were given life insurance policies (money paid to families if a family member dies). If a soldier died, his family would often use the life insurance policy to pay off their mortgage (a loan from a bank to buy a home). Many families lived on farms back then, so they would use the money to buy the farm. The phrase may also refer to the plot of land purchased in a graveyard for burial. Whatever the phrase refers to, it's a sad saying. Soldiers weren't making light of their friends' deaths when they used the saying. They were sad for them and scared that they would die too.

Luckily, Ethan's great-grandpa took the wheel and landed the plane safely in a field. He was scraped up and late to the wedding, but he survived to raise a family.

ALL THAT GLITTERS Isn't GOLD

Nina's school was having an end-of-year party in the gym on the last Friday before school got out. Nina's friends were planning to wear sequins on the day of the party.

Madison's mom bought her a sequined scarf. Mackenzie's mom bought her a sequined top. Hailey's mom bought her a sequined skirt. Nina's mom said, "A new outfit is not in the budget. Wear something you already have."

Instead, Nina spent forty dollars of her own money—which she'd been saving all year—on a pair of sequined leggings. The next day, the girls said they weren't wearing sequins after all. Mackenzie had washed her top, and now the sequins hung by threads.

Not all pretty, shiny objects are valuable. This sequined top shines, but the sequins fall off easily.

The same thing had happened to Hailey. Nina told her mother, who replied, "It's true what they say. All that glitters is not gold."

What did Nina's mom mean? **The saying *all that glitters is not gold* means that just because something looks valuable, it doesn't mean that it actually *is* valuable.** A similar phrase dates to the 1100s. Frenchman Alain de Lille wrote, "Do not hold everything gold that shines like gold." By the late Middle Ages (A.D. 500 to 1500), the phrase had changed into *all that glitters is not gold*. Similar phrases appear in several languages.

Nina decided to wear her sequined leggings to the party anyway. The next day, her mom showed her how to hand wash clothes so that sequins didn't come loose. Nina told her friends. They thought hand washing clothing sounded like a pain. They vowed never to buy sequins again!

These gold coins glitter a little—but just because something glitters, it doesn't mean it's gold.

The $64,000 Question

The math test was finally over, and so was the school day. Some kids ran for the buses to head home. Others gathered in the lunchroom for a scout meeting. Still others went to the soccer and baseball fields to practice after-school sports. Zach hung behind in the classroom as his teacher graded tests.

M ay I help you, Zach?" his teacher asked.

"Have you graded my test yet?" he replied.

"Yes," she said.

"How did I do?" he asked.

"That is the $64,000 question," she answered.

Zach wasn't sure what his teacher meant by that. All he knew was that she hadn't revealed whether he'd done OK or not. The suspense was really getting to him!

Awaiting answers to sixty-four-thousand-dollar questions usually *does* get to people. **That's because the phrase *$64,000 question* refers to hard questions—and questions for which people really want the answers.**

Host Hal March questions a contestant in a booth during the television game show *The $64,000 Question* in 1955.

Where did this phrase come from? <u>On the 1940s radio quiz show *Take It or Leave It*, contestants could win $2 if they answered very easy questions and $64 if they answered very hard questions.</u> (That isn't much money compared to today's game shows, but things cost less back then, so $64 was actually quite a bit of money.) Later, a television show modeled after the radio show upped the ante. It offered $64,000 for the hardest question. Subsequent game shows have offered even more. But *$64,000 question* remains the slang for a hard question. Sometimes people also say *$64,000,000 question*—probably because $64,000 isn't as much money as it used to be.

So what's the answer to Zach's $64,000 question? Did he ever get the info he'd waited so desperately after class to find out? Yes! His teacher took pity on him. "Good news, Zach," she finally said. "You got 98 percent. An A! I can't give you $64,000 for your grade. But I *am* proud of you!" Zach was pretty proud—and pretty relieved—himself.

Glossary

acquaintance: someone you have met but do not know well

ante: price, cost, or stakes

guild: a group representing the workers in a craft or trade

idiom: a commonly used expression or phrase that means something different from what it appears to mean

intertwined: connected or involved

life insurance policy: money paid to families if a family member dies

meteorology: the study of weather

mortgage: a loan from a bank to buy a home

origin: the cause or source of something, or the point where something began

parable: a story meant to teach a lesson or a moral

psychologist: one who studies the thoughts, emotions, and actions of people or animals. He or she may also try to help them be happier or lead better lives.

Further Reading

Bootman, Colin. *The Steel Pan Man of Harlem*. Minneapolis: Carolrhoda Books, 2009. This book is a fun takeoff on the story of the pied piper of Hamlin.

Doeden, Matt. *Put on Your Thinking Cap: And Other Expressions about School*. Minneapolis: Lerner Publications Company, 2013. Find out the meaning and the history behind thirteen fun school-related idioms.

Idioms and Their Meanings
http://www.buzzle.com/articles/idioms-and-their-meanings.html
Uncover new idioms in this list of the meanings and roots of idioms used in the United States.

Idioms by Kids
http://www.idiomsbykids.com
Check out more than one thousand kid-drawn pictures of the literal meanings of idioms. You can add your own examples too.

Idiom Site
http://www.idiomsite.com
Search this alphabetical list of idioms and their meanings.

Klingel, Cynthia. *Ack! There's a Bug in My Ear! (and Other Sayings That Just Aren't True)*. Mankato, MN: Child's World, 2008. This illustrated book sheds light on the meaning of several puzzling sayings.

Moses, Will. *Raining Cats and Dogs*. New York: Philomel Books, 2008. This picture book tells the story of different idioms against the backdrop of memorable illustrations.

Paint by Idioms
http://www.funbrain.com/funbrain/idioms
Test your knowledge of common idioms by taking the multiple-choice quizzes on this site from FunBrain.

Terban, Marvin. *In a Pickle and Other Funny Idioms*. New York: Clarion Books, 2007. This book uncovers the real meaning behind a number of everyday expressions.

———. *Scholastic Dictionary of Idioms*. Rev. ed. New York: Scholastic, 2006. Look up explanations for more than seven hundred idioms in this reference book with alphabetical listings and an index.

World Wide Words
http://www.worldwidewords.org/index.htm
Word scholar Michael Quinion writes articles and answers questions about words and expressions.

Index

Photo Acknowledgments

The images in this book are used with the permission of: © Andersen Ross/Blend Images/Getty Images, p. 5; © Preto Perola/Shutterstock.com, p. 6 (top); © iStockphoto.com/Terry J Alcorn, p. 6 (bottom); © KidStock/Blend Images/Getty Images, p. 7; © Marilyn Nieves/Vetta/Getty Images, p. 8; © Dmitriy Shironosov/Shutterstock.com, p. 10; © Simon Watson/Stone/Getty Images, p. 11; © Aleksandra Duda/Shutterstock.com, p. 12; © Eye Ubiquitous/SuperStock, p. 13; © Olga Vladimirova/Shutterstock.com, p. 14; © Photodisc/Getty Images, p. 15; © Oppenheim Bernhard/Digital Vision/Getty Images, p. 16; © Wealan Pollard/OJO Images/Getty Images, p. 17; © Tomas Sereda/Shutterstock.com, p. 18; © PjrStudio/Alamy, p. 19 (top); © Linda Hughes/Shutterstock.com, p. 19 (bottom); © FXQuadro/Shutterstock.com, p. 20; © Russell Shively/Shutterstock.com, p. 21; © Lew Robertson/Brand X Pictures/Getty Images, p. 22 (left); © iStockphoto.com/Selahattin Bayram, p. 22 (right); © Margaret Evans Price/Blue Lantern Studio/CORBIS, p. 23; © iStockphoto.com/R Sherwood Veith, p. 24; © Justin Paget/Photolibrary/Getty Images, p. 26; © Aleksandr Stennikov/Shutterstock.com, p. 27; © iStockphoto.com/Henrik Jonsson, p. 28; © CBS Photo Archive/Archive Photos/Getty Images, p. 29.

Front cover: © Mike Kemp/rubberball/Getty Images (bottom center); © iStockphoto.com/Alina Solovyova-Vincent (top center); © Gemenacom/Shutterstock.com (top right), (top left); © Vicente Barcelo Varona/Shutterstock.com (background); © prostophoto/Shutterstock.com (bottom left).

Main body text set in Adrianna Light 11/17.
Typeface provided by Chank.